CHICKENADE

4 Steps to Staying Motivated At Work, No Matter What Life Hands You

By Richard N. Stephenson

This book is about discovering the 4-step process to regaining control of motivation in your career and personal life. Take what life hands you and turn it into a more successful future.

TABLE OF CONTENTS

Published by RichardStep.com Publishing

Print Edition
http://richardstep.com

Chapter 1

When Life Hands You Chickens...

To say Harland Sanders had it tough for most of his life would not be doing the man justice. He was raised in an incredibly poor household and dropped out of elementary school to work.

As he passed into adulthood, Harland was never able to put down roots, and over the decades his list of "careers" included general farm laborer, army mule attendant, unsuccessful candidate for political office, and what was described as "amateur obstetrician."

Nothing lasted too long, and by the time he was in his forties, his list of jobs ran into the double digits

 The latest was running a service station where not many cars went for servicing. This gave Harland a lot of time to daydream of a better life.

One day he decided to start serving food. The station was so small that Harland had to prepare and serve everything in his backroom apartment.

Harland soon discovered he had a knack for whipping up a good meal, and before long the crush of food-only customers caused him to ditch the cars and concentrate on the restaurant. He moved the diner to a larger location and became a success in his hometown.

Now if that was the end of the story, I would not be telling it, for no one may have ever heard of Colonel Sanders. It gets better, but to do so it had to get worse first.

The restaurant stayed successful for more than a decade before a cruel twist of fate caused Harland Sanders' fortune to head downward. A new interstate was built that diverted traffic away from his restaurant. Business dried up and he went bankrupt at 65 years of age.

With his first social security check, Harland "Colonel" Sanders went with what he was good at and loved. He opened another restaurant.

Sanders 2.0 became a success and he was soon opening up one location after another. Pushing 70, Harland "Colonel" Sanders had finally arrived.

Making Chicken Work For You

How many times do you think the Colonel wanted to give up? As he was shoveling mule droppings, pulling weeds or wiping dipsticks, he must have wanted to scream at the top of his lungs "Get me out of here!"

Harland Sanders may have often (temporarily) felt sorry for himself. He may have even given up, again temporarily, as any man with well more than a dozen jobs in his adult life is likely to have done. Other people may have given up on him too at more than one of those jobs.

What if Harland Sanders stuck at one of those earlier jobs? What if he was made crew leader at the farm, or if he got another job within the army?

If Harland Sanders never experienced the failure he did, he would never get to enjoy the success that came later. Kentucky Fried Chicken (KFC) happened because others told him he was not good enough. Had he been the world's best weed puller, we would be without KFC and I'd have to make other dinner plans for this evening. Crispy, please!

One of the reasons Harland Sanders became successful was that after every failure, he got up and tried again. He may not have always known what he wanted, but he knew what he did not want. He went with his gut, recognizing that where his wandering mind went was an area worth exploring.

There are many lessons to glean from Harland Sanders' experience and they form the basis of this book. Never losing sight of those who rely on you, knowing yourself (what drives you, what you are good at, what defines you), and having a dream and the courage to follow it. Knowing how to properly follow it is key.

The lessons learned from all of these areas can be applied to anyone and to any situation, including yours. It's time to get you motivated at work and ready for a better future for your career.

It's time to own up to the 4-Steps to taking what life hands you and turning it into something you can use. When life hands you lemons, you make lemonade. When you can find the motivation to go and life is handing you chickens... you know what to do.

4-Steps to Chickenade:

- Step 1: Understand Your Goals
- Step 2: Find The Reasons Why
- Step 3: Learn To Change Today
- Step 4: Design Your Future Success

STEP 1

UNDERSTANDING YOUR GOALS

Chapter 2

Learning From Your Past

George Santayana said, "Those who cannot remember the past are condemned to repeat it." He was referring to people who repeat the same behaviors and processes over and over again and wonder why they are stuck in a rut, never progressing in life while others seem to get ahead. A problem many "stuck" people have is they are not very self-aware.

They seldom take time to think about whom they are, what they are good at, and what they enjoy. These people probably have some goals, but those goals are loosely defined, and are unaccompanied by the interim steps and objectives that are part of every plan to achieve those goals (more on that later). Because they are not that focused, they make rush decisions like quitting a perfectly good job for an opportunity that makes no sense.

Your past is over, but even if you are not proud of it, or if it features a bunch of seemingly unrelated positions, you can learn plenty that can help get a realistic picture of where you currently are and where you might wish to go. Before we look at your work history let's, look at your education.

Education History

What were your favorite subjects? Which ones were your least favorite? Few successful accountants hated mathematics and there are not too many writers who failed language arts. When you look back on your educational history, you are likely to see that your best subjects are related to the paths you chose to pursue.

On its own, this information may not say much to you. However, know that the goal is to generate a body of information that, when looked at all together, provides strong hints at career directions you will thrive in, which may very well include the one you are currently taking. This is the type of exploration we will do in this book.

How Do You Spend Your Free Time?

Another area you can glean much information from is your leisure time. These are the activities we *choose* to do.

Because they are by free choice, they are a much more accurate reflection of the types of experiences we actually enjoy, as opposed to tasks like work that can be influenced by location, money needs and other factors.

More important than the actual activity are some of its characteristics:

- Is it done indoors or outdoors?
- Is it done alone or in a group?
- Is it a physically demanding task or is it more sedentary?
- Does it take place in one location or do you have to go to multiple places?
- Is it intellectually challenging or does it to allow your mind to shut down a little and recharge?
- What are the specific tasks you do in these activities?

What you do for your recreation, and knowing why you do it, is especially important when you are unmotivated at work. One of the main purposes of recreation is to restore balance to our lives. If your job involves dealing with people all day, and you function best when there is more of a 50-50 split between dealing with people and working alone, you are going to seek activities that lean to the introverted side in order to restore your natural balance.

Remember the word "recreation," when broken down, means to "re-create" ourselves.

What we do in our off hours are not just random activities, but pastimes which provide experiences that are important to personality maintenance and development.

Spend some time looking at your hobbies and what you do in your free time. The answers will provide important clues to what activities you like most. If some of the clues point to the work you are currently doing, you need to do some soul searching as to why you are bored in your current position. This can be a stressful exercise, but always remember the end result is a happier and more fulfilled you. More to come on this topic later in the book.

Seek Out Trusted Opinions

Another way to learn about yourself is to talk to the people who know you best. Your family and friends spend the most time with you. After a while they will have naturally gathered a set of observations across different situations on what you are like.

No matter how self-aware you feel you are, you can be guaranteed some of these people will have impressions that will surprise you.

Ask them a series of questions:

- What tasks am I best at?
- Which ones do I struggle with?
- What am I doing when I am the happiest?
- If you were to hire me for any job, which one(s) would you hire me for and why?

Job Coaches' Favorite Trick

There is also a very practical method that resume developers and job coaches use when helping job seekers with little practical experience or who have large gaps in that experience. They cannot develop a traditional chronological resume, for prospective employers will soon see the breaks in their work history.

What the coaches do is have the job seeker take every task they have done, whether it is volunteer, household and childcare chores, or extracurricular activities at school, and list them on one side of a blank sheet of paper. Across from each entry the person lists every core activity involved in those roles.

Once completed, they look through the list for common traits in several of those activities. Certain ones tend to come up over and over again. The coach will take these groups of skills and, along with top school subjects, develop a resume that highlights the best while minimizing the areas that are not as strong.

What Motivates You At Work?

These tactics will get you started on learning about things you enjoy doing. The next step is to look at your goals. There are a host of tests and inventories online that you can work through that help identify what values are important to you.

A simple way to get yourself started is to rate yourself on the following statements on a scale of 1 to 6, where 1 is strongly disagree and 6 is strongly agree:

- My work must be intellectually challenging.
- I need variety in the day-to-day tasks of my job.
- The opportunity to be a leader at work is very important to me.
- I need to work around others most of the time.
- I need a high degree of security in my job.
- My ideal job is prestigious.
- I work best with little supervision.
- I need my work to be noticed.
- My job must allow me to spend a significant amount of time with my family and friends.
- My job must provide me with opportunities to learn and to grow.
- A large salary is important to me.

Look at which statements you give 5's and 6's to and ask yourself which types of jobs offer these combinations.

As you move through this book you should be generating a list of jobs that meet at least some of the criteria we have been discussing. The next step is to learn more about each specific one. You can do searches on the internet to learn some of the information, and those do play a role, but they are also often generic descriptions that do not allot for subcategories, geographic differences or a host of other factors.

The following sites are especially helpful here:

- **http://www.mynextmove.org**
- **http://www.bls.gov/emp/**
- **http://www.bart.gov/about/jobs/descriptions**

Talk To Those Who Know

The best way to learn about the job is to talk to someone who is actually doing it. Do you know anyone in that job? How about your family and friends? Do they know anyone? Are there business networking events in your area where you can mingle with different people?

Many fields also have professional associations that promote the types of careers available in that sector. They should have literature or website information to provide. Many hold regular social events and have volunteer opportunities available where you can experience that environment.

Have you considered part time employment in that line of work? Maybe you can work an evening per week and on a day off. You make a little extra money and get firsthand knowledge on whether or not this is a career you should consider.

As you are using these strategies, look for people who excel in the role - those who are successful, who have moved up, won awards and who have their colleagues' respect. Watch how they work, what they prioritize and how the organize their time. Ask them for lunch and talk about their education, what they like about the job, what they dislike, and future prospects. As you are listening, keep your "must have" lists from earlier in your mind.

Mentors: The Career-Makers

Keep these people's contact information close by, because if you choose to pursue the line of work they are in, they may make a good mentor for you. Mentors are people who have accumulated a significant amount of information on a given subject, who are seen as good at what they do, and who are willing to share that information with you.

Many successful people from across the job spectrum credit their mentors with providing the crucial difference between success and failure in their career. While friends and family are caring and supportive, no one knows the travails of what you are going through more than someone who has been through the same trials and who has succeeded.

Time and time again these people recall a specific piece of advice their mentor shared, or a story that clearly showed the mentor knew what they were going through. The shared experience is a powerful tool and mentors can provide it better than anyone else.

Successful mentors have generated a list of best practices that you will probably not find in any textbook. These are real life strategies that have worked in actual situations. Many are generated by trial and error. These will be some of the most valuable pieces of information a mentor can provide.

There's a hilarious scene in the movie Back to School, starring Rodney Dangerfield. He is a successful businessman who decides to go to college so he can spend time with his son. One professor does not have much actual business experience. One day this professor lists all of the steps one takes in securing a building for your business.

Rodney Dangerfield's character interrupts the stodgy professor and adds a whole list of other expenses, such as costs related to schmoozing the building inspector. The students copy his information and the teacher gets increasingly flustered.

Please don't think the moral of this story is to bribe your way to the top! It is here to illustrate the value of practical experience that can only be given by someone who has been there.

Putting It All Together

So far you have spent time in self-assessment, talking to other people who know you, breaking down your experience, and learning from others. Now it is time to plan out how much work it will take to become employed in the different fields that interest you.

Sometimes when you are at the beginning of a new stage in life, the end seems so far away but it's really not. When you take your ultimate goal and break it down into several smaller steps it makes the process much more manageable. Here are several parts you can break your job goal into:

1. Education

- Do you already have the education you need to move into this new field?
- If you do not, can you take the training at a school near where you live or will you have to relocate?
- Can you relocate?
- Is the training available in the evenings, part time or by correspondence?
- Can you afford the cost or will you have to borrow money?
- How can you effectively change the family budget to accommodate the added cost of education and potential loss of income?
- If you have family responsibilities, can others help?
- Does your current employer pay for skills development?

2. Getting Experience

- Can you get part time employment in your desired field while going to school?
- What are the job prospects like locally upon graduation?
- Will you have to relocate and is that a realistic option for you?
- What is the wage scale like for entry level positions?
- How can you adjust your family budget to reflect this new wage?

Learn from your past, prepare for a better future in or out of where you're at, and align yourself with true internal motivation. Now let's look at our skills and accomplishments and how they come into play.

Chapter 3

Happy Home Or Time To Move?

Whether we are happy or not in our job, it makes sense to periodically take stock of our performance. Publicly listed companies issue quarterly reports so shareholders can see how their investments are performing and what the future holds. Many companies schedule regular performance reviews with their employees.

You do not have to wait for someone else to initiate a performance review for you. Complete your own by honestly looking at your output at work. Take your job description, or create one if you have to, and see how well you meet or surpass its details.

A self-review comes with the added advantage of being able to assess personal goals you do not wish to share with any employer. The information we have talked about so far in this book forms a good basis for any review.

If you are completely honest with yourself, one answer you might not be prepared for is that your current position is not that bad.

Maybe your disenchantment is because of conflict with a co-worker, a personal issue outside of work, or because you like the company but feel stuck in your role, yet you have not discussed changing that role with anybody.

Human resource people and counselors bemoan how often workers opt for a drastic change when a simple one could have achieved the desired results. A person often leaves a perfectly fixable situation for fear of upsetting someone.

Performance reviews let you catch yourself before you go too far off track, and also allow you to celebrate the little victories along the way. Knowing your starting point is the only way you can determine how long it might take to reach the goals you have set for yourself.

If you determine you need a change of scenery, you must have an exit plan. Most people cannot just get up and quit their current job so they can devote 100% of their time to their dreams. Mortgages, the need to eat and other expenses necessitate having to stay where you are, at least for a while.

Go For The Gold

How do you make the most of this time? Try maximizing the positive aspects of your current job by seeing if you can focus on certain skills you can transfer to your desired career. Look for opportunities to gain experience that make you a more attractive candidate in that new field.

Let's take what we've learned so far and apply it to your current position.

The first area we looked at was favorite school subjects. If your favorite area was mathematics, seek out opportunities to help with inventory, cash or financial reporting.

If you enjoy communicating with others, look for opportunities to write for the company newsletter, answer e-mails or to produce something for the company Facebook page.

Fill in for the customer service staff on breaks or holidays. Offer to serve on Christmas party committees or to help at career fairs or trade shows.

Previously, you considered your favorite pastimes and broke them down into specific aspects you enjoyed that you can look for in an ideal job.

Are there opportunities to work more inside or outside the company or can you change the physical nature of what you do?

How about tasks that alter your level of intellectual stimulation? Can you work at multiple locations?

Your friends and family gave you feedback on your strengths. Can you incorporate those? Are you even sure what your strengths are?

I've got a free Strengths Test for you if you don't. It would be a great breather-break to take it now and get your top 5 strengths (and 1 weakness!) in mind.

http://bit.ly/freestrengthstest

We learned about common workplace motivators and you took a survey where you answered questions on a six point scale. Take the statements you scored with either a five or a six and look for opportunities for growth at work.

Seek to get more or less intellectual stimulation, a different amount of variety, develop leadership skills, work more with others or alone, get more or less acclaim, and to learn about new areas, whether it be by working in another department or by going to employer-sponsored schooling.

By taking your favorite school subjects, hobbies, what motivates you at work and what others see as your strongest areas, you have tools you can use to make the remainder of your time at your current job productive while increasing your qualifications for that new career.

Think of it as on the job training (OJT) for the next "J" while doing good work at the current "J."

STEP 2

FIND THE REASONS WHY

Chapter 4

When Maslow Speaks, You Listen

Abraham Maslow was a noted psychologist who made many contributions to our understanding of the human mind. He is best known for his hierarchy of needs, a concept with some similarities to the workplace motivators discussed in chapter two.

The hierarchy of needs states there are five levels of needs people have. Before we can seek to meet the needs in a higher level, we must first provide for the more basic needs from the ones below.

Level 5 consists of self-actualization needs. Most can be at least partially reached through securing a job that makes best use of our skills, abilities and interests. They consist of our desires for self-fulfillment and peak experiences.

According to Maslow, we have to first meet our more basic needs before we aspire to self-actualization. The initial level is populated by basic survival requirements such as food, shelter and rest. Once those are secured, we seek stability and a societal order, with reasonable limits attached to our actions.

We are fortunate to live in a society where most of these first two levels are present for the majority of us. In the third level, the individual strives for a sense of belonging within different groups. We yearn to feel loved and respected by our family, our community, and our work group.

Our relationships at work play important roles in our social and career development, but , when healthy, they also ensure our continued ability to provide for the earlier stage needs like shelter, food and safety of not only ourselves but also for those who depend on us, like our children, spouses, and in some cases our parents.

Motivation By Hierarchy

I include this because knowing why we work and reminding ourselves of who depends on us is a powerful motivator to secure and maintain productive employment. We are more likely to withstand job pressures if we put them in the proper place on the pecking order, which is below the importance of our loved ones having food, clothing and shelter.

Those pressures may make us feel like quitting, but because we accept the responsibility of caring for those for whom we are responsible, we do not succumb to the pressure to flee. We instead seek solutions. This may include looking for new work while keeping the current job or working to find a solution that allows us to stay in our current position because we enjoy the work, the company, or for other reasons.

Keeping proper motivation can make all the difference in our attitude, which shapes how we view our situation and how we choose to act within it. Former professional wrestler Ted DiBiase, now a preacher and public speaker, tells a story of going to visit war veterans from Iraq and Afghanistan who were rehabilitating their injuries at Walter Reed Military Hospital.

One gentleman had lost three limbs in service and was about to lose the last one. He was beyond despondent and was losing his sense of purpose and hope for living. The many, many shocks of war, which were continuing even after he arrived stateside, were proving too much for him to handle.

One day, someone was visiting with the man during a particularly bleak period and asked him who was in the picture he had taped by his bedside. He said it was his wife and began breaking down uncontrollably.

For reasons we can all empathize with, the man forgot about someone who loved him unconditionally and who needed him in her life. That breakdown was his low point, and with her in mind, he began furiously rehabilitating his injuries. He now works at Walter Reed as an encourager to the other veterans who are regaining their health.

Losing track of where we are happens to everyone over the course of their lifetime. That is why it is so important to be constantly aware of your personal situation so you can avoid these detours completely or to get back on the proper path as soon as possible.

Maslow's Evaluation And You

One way successful people do this is by periodically going through self-evaluations that mirror the one detailed in chapter three, except they look at all areas of life, not just work. We can model our personal review on Maslow's hierarchy.

Start with yourself.

- Are you eating properly?
- Are you getting enough rest?
- Do you regularly exercise?
- How are things going for you at work (think back to previous examples in this book)?

It may sound selfish, but you must start with yourself. Your personal health is the foundation upon which every role you engage in (employee, parent, spouse, etc.) and every action you undertake is built. You may be able to fool everyone for a while, but ultimately you cannot give from an empty tank and all of your relationships and outputs will suffer.

Then it is time to look at your most important relationships. If you are married, it is your spouse. After that it is your children.

- Are you sufficiently providing for your family?
- Are your loved ones' core needs being met?
- Are you spending enough quality time with them?
- Are you showing genuine love and concern for them?

The answers to this next question can be uncomfortable. What if you are spending many hours at work, so you can pay the mortgage and for all of the kids' activities? Is your family getting to see *enough* of you? This is something I have to deal with daily and it can really hurt if left unchecked.

Is the trade-off between a slightly higher lifestyle worth missing quality experiences with those closest to you? Your motivations may be noble, but be honest with yourself when you ask whether or not your family has **all** of you *often enough*.

- Are you having fun together?
- What is all this work for anyway?

Assuming you have the basic needs of shelter, food and safety met, you can begin to think about chasing the higher needs Maslow describes. The fourth level is called "esteem needs." These include self-esteem, confidence, achievement, respect *of* others and respect *by* others.

You may be looking at that list and thinking about how many of those can be met through a positive work experience. They all can be met at work, but they can also be met in our leisure time. Having these needs met through more than one area of our life insulates us from the damage losing that one area could have.

If our entire self-worth rests on our work identity, what happens if we lose our job or when we retire? In such a scenario, we could feel left with nothing which can be damaging to our psyche and our relationships.

As long as we are alive, we have leisure time. As we discussed earlier, recreation breaks down to "re-create," which means it plays an important restorative role for us. Recreation also injects much needed balance into our lives.

It gives us opportunities to participate in behaviors which are not present in our work and home lives. Opportunities to learn new skills, to be good at something, and to develop additional social relationships are other important benefits.

Recreation is also supposed to be fun. We need to have reasonable amounts of fun in our lives. The expectation of fun provides a much needed break from work or family responsibilities, and inserts a gap into what can look like a never ending list of duties.

Having a game, movie night, jog or even a good book to look forward to at the end of the work day gives us something to anticipate. In this "break from responsibility," we replenish our reserves and recharge ourselves for the next set of obligations.

These mental breaks cannot happen willy-nilly, they have to be part of your financial budgeting, goal setting and periodic evaluations. Short term, that means making dedicated "me time." Longer term, it means budgeting for the costs of that activity, which includes time, money, and capabilities. A regular news item is how most Americans are failing to adequately plan for retirement.

While most of the pieces focus on financial planning, the same can be said of planning for how we are going to spend (and pay for) our free time. Many people dream of traveling the world but retire only to find they are lucky enough to pay the bills each month. Incorporate your favorite activities into your long range planning and start directing your future instead of worrying about it.

Chapter 5

For The Love Of Experience And Integrity

By this point, you have an idea of how to create a plan that will result in a happier working you. At some level this plan will involve new experiences, as at minimum you will be transitioning from a less than ideal situation to a happier one. Whether you hope to move across the hall or across the country, you have a goal that takes you away from the situation you are currently in.

Chances are you will not automatically pop into that ideal situation tomorrow, so there will be a waiting period until you are able to move forward. That delay may be while you wait for an opening in another department within your company, another company in your field, or an entirely new field with its own set of possibilities. It may be because you have to get more experience or education first.

Maximize your time where you are now while preparing for tomorrow.

Regardless of your goal, concentrate on improving your productivity. Say you produce 10 widgets per hour, shoot for 15. You average three sales per shift, why not aim for five? Perhaps your tips average $50 per night. Strive to improve your service level so you bring home another $20 on top of that.

Whether this limbo period is a week or if it is a year, you are choosing each work period to focus on the immediate (with an eye to the future of course) and worrying about what you can control at that very moment.

You are not distracting yourself with wondering why the phone is not ringing or why you are not in your dream job. A key trait most successful people share is their ability to minimize, and often eliminate, the time they spend on factors over which they have no control. It is wasted time.

Two things happen when you focus on improving your performance:

#1 - You Improve

Slashing the preparation time for restaurant meals if you are a line cook means customers get their food quicker, which makes them happier, which makes the chances of them returning higher, which makes your boss happier. It also means tables open up quicker, leading to more people getting to eat, and finally to more profit for the restaurant.

Whether your goal is to stay with that restaurant and move up or if it is to transition into a completely new field, you have accomplished a few important things that bring that goal closer. The first is you have an important addition to your resume. Stating you have cut your preparation time or improved your sales rate by 20% looks impressive no matter what field you aspire to be in.

What business doesn't need someone who is aware of the importance of efficiency, who can create a plan to become more efficient, execute, and then evaluate that plan? That is about as transferable and as universal of a skill as there is. Every employer will be impressed by that achievement, especially in this age where having quantifiable deliverables on your resume is so important.

#2 - You Get Noticed

While this is not a given, if you have taken steps to improve your performance and have done better, chances are supervisors and co-workers have seen it. If you get regular performance reviews, then you must discuss these goals.

Why else is this important? The biggest reason is integrity. Ultimately, we all have to answer to ourselves and our conscience about our work effort. If you value yourself, you should hold yourself to a high standard.

Push yourself, challenge yourself to grow, and expect more from your performance. As you have a plan and goals from earlier in the book, inject some balance and pat yourself on the back for your successes when you conduct your regular review. Those with integrity always stand out.

Another more practical reason is to gain references. You need good references to be able to get any job. That co-worker you traded shifts with or that supervisor you worked overtime for is more likely to give you a good referral because you made the effort to make their job easier. They are especially crucial if you want to move up in your current company, as commentary becomes part of your work file and will outlive staff that leaves.

These people are more likely to help you in many ways because you extended the effort to help them. They will be a reference. Each person in your business network is an extra set of eyes that can let you know about job opportunities they hear about through their contacts. The hidden job market is where many of the best opportunities are and contacts that have firsthand knowledge of your ability are your best way to break into it.

People will not recommend you if you appear to be lackluster as it will look bad on them. Any employer accepting a recommendation from a staff member or friend about you will pay closer attention to that recommendation than they will to a resume in the mail. You have a connection to someone who they have seen and is credible in their own eyes. Some of that credibility gets automatically transferred to you.

No matter how wide the gulf is between where you are and where you want to be there are always some skills you can work on at your current job. In addition to efficiency, look for opportunities to improve your abilities in supervising and staff training, cross-training, teamwork, customer service , problem solving and finances. These are skills that are good in most jobs and will carry you forward.

STEP 3

LEARN TO CHANGE TODAY

Chapter 6

Learning To Gel With Yourself And Others

In Chapter 5, we recognized there is a high probability you will not be able to simply snap your fingers and create a work environment that inspires and motivates you. We started off with looking at ways you can motivate yourself internally by setting goals and focusing on areas over which you exert control.

Now that we have addressed the internal motivation side of things, it is time to switch to the external. Let's look at your work environment and your co-workers for ways you can increase your level of interest at work. Your physical environment is a significant influence on how productive and happy you are at work. As I am writing this I keep switching my 'happy' and 'productive' modes back and forth.

Think about how it feels when you have finished a major project and task that you have worked hard on. It feels good, doesn't it? That is why so many people are attracted to gardening, home improvement, and even artistic endeavors in their spare time. The satisfaction of seeing positive results from your labors feeds the soul and is a shot of energy to our spirit. It makes us feel good.

The reverse is also true. When I am happiest at work, I am more productive. Normally, this is when I've had several good nights of sleep, I enjoy my team's company and I am excited to get to work. Most people are wired this way. Even the lazier ones have, at their core, the desire to matter and to produce.

Our physical work environment makes it hard sometimes. Whether it is the actual location, the layout, or other factors, there are a host of areas we can look at individually to see if there are steps we can take to make our work area more conducive to producing valuable results.

Where exactly is your work space? Is it in a high traffic area where co-workers and customers frequently go by? Some people thrive on social interaction and find it stimulates their creativity and productivity. After too much time alone, they leave their space and seek others out for a bit of a recharge.

Others are the opposite. The noise breaks their concentration and repeatedly forces them to repeat steps. They know it's unproductive and they may be under the pressure of a deadline or from superiors who expect a higher level of output.

If you are distracted by background noise, people coming into your workspace or the phone ringing, you may be an auditory learner. One of the three major learning styles, auditory learners literally retain information the best through processing external sounds.

Are You An Auditory Learner?

If you answer yes to many of the following questions you probably are.

- Do you read slowly?
- Does it take a long time for you to interpret complex pictures or detailed graphs?
- Do you enjoy talking to others?
- Are you a music fan, with a great memory for lyrics and bands?
- Do you prefer giving oral reports more than written ones?

There are several tactics auditory learners use to increase their productivity at work. If possible, they get a workspace away from as much noise as possible, somewhere not close to telephones, elevators or machinery.

They can also request ear plugs or noise cancelling headphones to cancel out external noise.

Even a space with a door to shut when they need to concentrate can do wonders. Receiving training manuals in audio format on a CD or as MP3's for their smartphones, and having a device to record meetings or other events that relay information important to their role, can greatly help the auditory learner retain information.

Other People Are Visual Learners

If you see yourself in many of the following statements, then you may very well be a visual learner.

- Are you good at spelling but forgetful of names?
- Do you like pictures and charts?
- Do you like bold colors?
- Do you pay much attention to your fashion?
- Are you a hand talker?
- Do you take detailed notes?
- When people speak, do you make movies in your mind of their descriptions?

Visual learners have many strategies available to boost their performance. After a meeting with others, many visual learners find it beneficial to "decompress."

They find a place where they will not be distracted and then let the information filter in. They need to do this because their natural inclination tends to watching more than listening.

If you are a visual learner, take detailed notes and ask for written materials, meeting minutes, manuals and other visual information you can refer to when needed.

Where you are situated during meetings can also help. Try and get a spot where you can see the main speaker head on. That visual prompt helps the mind process information. This tactic also translates to one-on-one discussions.

If you are in a work environment where people yell requests across the shop floor or from around corners, this may make it more difficult to process important information. Try having those discussions face-to-face, and watch the person's body language for important clues. This helps many people.

If you are involved with a big project that consists of many steps, make a map or critical path of the steps you need to take.

Such devices provide a nice visual recipe for you as you work your way through the process.

Because visual is your predominant learning style, seeing the map triggers your creativity and stimulates the thought patterns that allow you to produce your best work in the shortest period of time.

And Then There Were Tactile Learners

These people are the ones who are always moving around and who are the ball of energy at work. Tactile learners chafe at having to sit through long presentations. If someone is a toe tapper or a pacer at meetings, chances are they are a tactile learner. Do you answer 'yes' to many of the following statements?

- I like having the radio on when I work (especially to keep me moving).
- I enjoy doing two things at once.
- I often pace during meetings, or wish I could.
- I enjoy acting and visual arts.
- I am good at sports.
- My eye-hand coordination is above average.
- When I am learning something new, I roll up my sleeves and throw myself right into the middle of it.

If this is you, try and create a work environment where you can move around often. Should you find yourself in a long day of meetings or desk bound, take your gym clothes and go for a jog or lengthy walk over lunch hour. Let the information filter in, or even have recorded meeting minutes, audio manuals or books playing on your music device.

Take frequent breaks when digesting large amounts of material and make sure you walk around at a minimum. Much like the visual learner who needs a map or the audio learner who processes information by talking to others, the motion of you getting up and moving around stimulates your mind and puts it in the environment where it best retains and produces information.

Additional Considerations

In the twenty-first century, we are more sensitive than ever about making accommodations for persons with disabilities in the workplace. Along with this awareness comes a long list of devices and tools that can be employed that allow a person with a disability to make the same contributions as anyone else.

Glare reducing screens, Braille communications and proper lighting can be employed for persons with visual impairments. Simple modifications to office furniture, equipment and floor plans are a tremendous help for persons with a wide range of physical limitations.

If you have some physical or mental considerations that are impacting your ability to produce like you know you can, consult your company benefits plan, as many cover consultations with occupational therapists and other professionals that can help you through what can be an uncomfortable situation.

There are many social service agencies that specialize in helping people with physical and mental impairments thrive at their workplace. These organizations have the specialized knowledge of your area of need, along with evidence of how applying sensible solutions allows you to become a more productive employee. They can serve as your advocate and will work to educate your company about your strengths and needs.

This knowledge can only take it so far and the rest is up to you. Do not assume that others are as receptive to this information as you are. Be prepared to advocate for yourself by taking steps that allow you to succeed. Ask for certain accommodations. Be assertive but kind in telling people you need some time alone to process what you have just heard or to work on an important assignment.

Applying The External

Take everything you have read so far in this chapter and think about the people you work with. Who are the auditory learners? Which people like to be in a group, ask questions frequently, and get distracted by noise when they need to work alone?

If you have to work closely with an auditory learner, remember to describe what you want them to do in an in-person or telephone conversation. You may mean well by stopping by to share some piece of news, but if an auditory learner is in the middle of an important project, try and save the bit for a break.

We've all worked with people who can't stop fidgeting and have a hard time staying still. These people are in constant overdrive. Allow these tactile learners the chance to participate in new product demonstrations, or to take one home or back to their office so they can master it. Recognize their need to get up and move not as rudeness but something they need to do to concentrate.

How about that person with a workplace injury or disability who you work with? How can you change your work pattern to assist them? Carrying heavy items, speaking clearly or allowing for extra time for certain difficult tasks can make a world of difference to someone who has to deal with barriers the rest of us do not.

Working Well With Others

Two basic human needs are to be understood and appreciated. When you illustrate to others that you are trying to adapt your behavior in order to better understand them and you want to help them succeed, you create bonds that will often allow for a better work environment. Many times you will find they will make the extra effort to help you too.

Social interactions are another important way that people learn about each other and develop empathy. Does your workplace have a social committee or a company sports team?

Use this as an opportunity to get to know people in other departments. Pretty soon Bob in Accounting is not just a voice on the phone asking you to get your receipts in on time.

He is a guy who gets frustrated because he spends half of his time chasing down people who are late in submitting their paperwork. This gets him heat from *his* boss. Mary in the head office is occasionally late because she has a child with special needs who has to go to many doctor appointments.

Some companies allow for periodic staff exchanges so people see the needs of different areas and how they fit into the corporate whole. Developing an understanding for the challenges faced by another department makes you better able to be a good coworker to them and for them to be one to you.

Cooperating With Company Culture

Now that you have a heightened sense of awareness of how you and your coworkers learn, look at your workplace culture. A company style always develops, whether that is a highly social one in a sales or service industry that favors go-getters or a more informal one dictated by the star performers, supervisors, or other opinion-leaders who have a prominent role in the company.

Is there a predominant learning style favored by most people in your company? Is the company populated by extroverts? A strong introvert working amongst extroverts may have to struggle to get heard above the noise. An extroverted work environment may also be a highly social one where staff go out together or have each other over to their homes.

- Are you participating in that kind of event?
- Are you getting invited out?

Company business can get done at parties and social ties can be strengthened that can lead to people getting promoted before you. If you work in this type of situation, then it may be good for your career to head out every once in a while and genuinely enjoy it. Stretch yourself!

If many of your coworkers are married with young children, they may not have time for out-of-work interactions, especially on weeknights. Organizing more family-oriented events may be one way to get to know other people and to understand their situations.

You can also take a practical, ABC's approach to assessing your workplace. What are the key positions at work that get the most responsibility and attention? What are the company priorities and who is in charge of them? Who are the stars in the company and what traits do they possess?

Tough Questions To Ask

By knowing the company "personality," the workplace culture, and the top skills and character traits of the best performers, you should have a good idea of the qualities your company prioritizes. How many of these do you have? Are you a good match for your workplace culture? Do you have similar morals and values?

Are others passing you on the corporate ladder? Are they a better match with the company's optimal skill set than you are? If so, look for opportunities to improve your weaker skills on the job or to get education outside the workplace. Does your company pay for training?

If your skill set is fine, how good of a self-advocate are you? Do the decision makers know how valuable you are to your company? Are you in regular communication with your supervisors? Are you getting proper credit for the work you do?

Some people seem dusted by gold. They are always in the right place at the right time. The good luck follows them around. Some are indeed fortunate, but many more are very conscious about taking care of their career path and placing themselves in situations where their accomplishments are noticed. This often involves studying the personalities of the decision makers (read: communication styles) to determine when and how to best communicate their achievements and best points.

Chapter 7

A Big To-Do About Habits

So much of what we have talked about so far in this book revolves around determining what factors in your environment you have control over. Success lies in understanding your preferred learning style and that of your coworkers, assessing the workplace culture, developing empathy for those around you, and setting meaningful goals.

If you follow all of these steps, then you become more effective because you are not wasting time on issues whose outcomes you cannot affect. You develop a focus. Because you are prioritizing manageable tasks, you get more done, and your confidence goes up.

You cannot lose! If you get noticed at work, your reviews should improve, relations with coworkers get better and new opportunities open up.

If none of these things occur, you have developed a new focus you can take with you to the next opportunity. This chapter continues down this road of learning more about yourself.

Getting In The Rhythm Of Work

Another aspect of yourself that you should know is your work rhythm. What times of the day are you most alert and productive? Which days of the week and periods of the year are you at your best?

If you're not a morning person, there is nothing worse than bumping into the office eager beaver before you've had your morning coffee. They're full of energy and super happy. They cannot wait to get going.

Good for them. But that's not you. Maybe you need that caffeine to head through your system. You spend the first section of your Monday morning setting up your week, answering emails, or doing other light duties to warm yourself up. By morning break you are ready to go. Before you know it is time to head home.

Chances are, if you chart these periods over a few months you will notice certain trends. Keep track of your moods, energy levels and the quality of the work you produce at different parts of the day. When is your best work produced? When is your lower quality work generated? Are there times when you feel like being around people more than others?

Now look at the requirements of the job. If there are certain times of the day when you absolutely have to be somewhere, there is nothing you can do about that. The rest of the time you can do something about. If you are one of those people who needs a bit of time to get going in the morning, avoid scheduling big meetings or client appointments during those periods.

If you have an office scheduler, block off certain times of the day so you can get specific tasks done. If your creative peak is between 10:00 AM and 2:00 PM, schedule team meetings and your idea development time then. Try and place any mandatory commitments outside your peak productivity periods. Try and leave your mundane tasks for your lower energy periods.

Many people in customer service who work an extra hour here or there will say they get more done in the 90 minutes they stay late and the doors are locked than they do in the eight hours they are paid to be there. That is because they are free from distractions and can focus on one task without interruption.

Mastering The To-Do List

Another way to stay focused and be productive is by keeping a "to do" list and updating it regularly as tasks get done and new ones get assigned. If you know the job well, you can probably predict some duties well before they happen. Add them to that list too.

Getting them done well in advance makes you look good, shows you have a "good feel" for the role, and positions you well to handle the surprises that pop up in every job as you have the extra time through your effective planning.

There are always times when you find yourself with a spare hour or two, say at the end of the week or during a down time in your industry's business cycle. That is the time to complete those housekeeping duties and other tasks that you may not enjoy but have to attend to. Getting them done during these slow periods increases the chances of you being able to do what you most enjoy during your most productive times.

Stop Fooling Around Already

The converse of all of this is you should also know when you tend to get lazy and are more likely to fool around on time wasting activities such as computer games, social media sites and other activities unrelated to work. Many companies block such sites and others have mechanisms in place that allow people to monitor your computer activity.

They say idle hands are the devil's workshop. If you know there are certain times you are most prone to fooling around (from the handy activities outlined earlier), schedule some important activities during that time, or take your breaks. Have coffee with a co-worker, or do something that rejuvenates you, like going for a short walk.

What can start out as a game or two on a website, or some idle net surfing, can quickly become a serious issue that can derail your career. Professional counselors confirm the many cases of people who have lost their jobs because of accessing pornography at work, gambling online, or spending too much time on social media.

No one wakes up one day and says they are going to spend so much time on objectionable websites at work just to lose their job. It starts subtly and grows over time. If you believe this may be an issue for you, there are accountability websites where you can register your name and the email address of a friend.

That friend will get a message whenever you visit a suspect site. Depending on the site you choose, your accountability partner will also get a time stamp and link to the pages you visited. I'll leave the Google searching to you as there are a ton of resources ranging from to-do list enforcement help to "unwholesome video" addiction busting.

Regardless, choose your accountability partner wisely. This person must be reliable and someone you are comfortable sharing details of your life with. They should have a good work ethic themselves, as it does not do much good if they see your suspect site and raise you two more.

You can also easily block sites on your home computer by entering one simple line of code. Do an internet search on "blocking sites in (name of your operating system)." It only takes a few minutes and is one of the most productive ways to eliminate time wasters from your work life.

STEP 4

DESIGN YOUR FUTURE SUCCESS

Chapter 8

Your Motivations And Surrounding Goals

Back in Chapter 2 we discussed common workplace motivators, the characteristics everyone needs present in their work in order for it to be satisfying. You answered a short series of questions on a six-point scale, with a score of 5 or 6 meaning that trait most likely needs to be present in order for you to get fulfillment from your work. Internal motivators include social interaction, intellectual stimulation, variety, attention, supervision, salary, prestige, professional development and free time away from work.

Over the first 7 chapters of this book we looked at different aspects of workplace motivation, and several similarities have come up during the process. They can be boiled down to "know yourself" and "know the work."

- What are your four most important motivators?
- Are they present in your current job?
- Can they somehow be added to your job if they are not?

If you're not sure what your motivators are, then I've got another quiz for you. Take the free Self-Motivation Quiz and figure out how the top 9 motivators rank for you.

http://richardstep.com/self-motivation-quiz-test/

It is important to clarify this as soon as possible. Start with ways in which you could possibly increase the presence of your important workplace motivators in your current role. Can you carve out a new position for yourself by taking on additional areas of responsibility? Showing initiative by sharing higher aspirations with your superiors can be seen as a positive step.

I say "can" because if to date your performance has been suspect, management may frame your desire for a bigger role as simply a play for more money or prestige, without the needed performance to back it up. Before you consider approaching management with such an offer, take an honest look at your own performance to make sure the solid foundation for increased responsibility is present.

Making It Work With What You Have

If you have that good base, you are at an advantage. Companies like to promote from within, because they are giving critical responsibilities to a known commodity. Some promotions can satisfy the needs of people's internal motivators, as they come with responsibilities that increase your prestige, pay and responsibility levels. They may also be an instant cure for the lethargy that can develop after someone has been in the same role for a while (the lethargy is good, as it is a signal for change).

Be careful, for as promotions giveth, they also taketh away. While your salary and prestige may increase, the position probably removes you from your work social group and could necessitate overtime and you being on call. Is the exchange worth it?

If you determine there is no way to get your needs met from your current job, then it is best to accelerate your search for a new position that does satisfy those internal motivators. Be careful how much of your job search is done at work, as you should want to finish strong and receive a good reference.

It is also important to assess how well your workplace motivators match your goals. Many people think the two are the same, but they can be very different if you are not that self-aware. People who enjoy the work of producing the widget earn a promotion or start their own company only to find they are no longer creating anything.

Now they are spending their time on the telephone, in meetings, and supervising other people who are building the items they used to enjoy producing. They also have less time to spend those summer weekends with the family as they are on call. Not to discount owning your own company, but there's plenty to know before you leap.

Remember to think long and hard about your goals, and make sure they mesh well with your personal motivators. As the above example shows, everyone could use some extra money but overtime may not be worth it if that pay bump comes at the expense of factors that attracted you to the work in the first place.

Internally Focused Goals

There are two distinct types of goals you should keep in mind while considering your future. Internal focus goals are those aims that are part of your core. Closely related to your internal motivators, these are the ones that really drive you, that, when present and accessed, give you that sense of focus and passion.

They later contribute to your satisfaction of a job well done. A writer truly knows when they have produced good work - they do not need a good review or a spot on a top ten list to tell them so. So does the tradesperson, the waiter and any other person who really knows what it takes to succeed in their line of work.

Know your internal focus goals and know them well, for the world is full of people who can bring you down if you let them. Some people want something for nothing. Others are unreasonable, never satisfied and will complain no matter what you do.

We all know people who, for whatever reason, are unhappy with their lot in life and take that out on others. Conservatives who did not "go for it" in their desired career may, out of jealousy, try and bring down those who took the risk.

Be careful who you share your hopes and goals with, as the world is full of critics but short on people who truly respect you and know what makes you tick. At several points in this book we have discussed mentors and accountability partners. Here is another time when they can help.

The accountability partner has established they care about you as a person. The mentor may as well, but has also walked the walk you are currently on, and knows the best practices and common pitfalls related to your field.

Externally Focused Goals

The other types of goals are external focus goals. These are items that are at least partially in the hands of other people, so do not measure your self-worth on them.

External focus goals can nicely augment your short-term plan by providing an achievable milestone to measure your performance against.

Perhaps last month it took you an average of 6 hours per day to complete your service route or to finish a rotation. Try for five and one-half hours this month. Maybe there is a company award you can chase.

External focus goals are important whether or not we are satisfied in our work. Those considering a change can put their attention toward an external focus goal such as getting a positive review at year end, having a major project completed by a certain date, or completing a reorganization of the filing system before leaving for another job.

It takes your attention off what can be a difficult situation and repositions it onto some aspect of the job you can affect. Focusing on the manageable can increase our confidence and happiness through the increased probability of achievable outputs solely reliant on our efforts.

Chapter 9

Your Motivation Living Plan

Now we can put together a comprehensive plan consisting of every area covered in the first eight chapters. We have looked at a large amount of ground, so putting everything in one place may help you keep track of the information as you customize a plan that works for you.

This is a "living plan," meaning you will be constantly referring to it as you go about its steps. Some of the areas, like assessing how you are caring for yourself and your loved ones and contact with your mentors and accountability partners, are ongoing processes.

Remember earlier when I wrote about how plans do not necessarily veer off track suddenly, that they are more likely to gradually veer off over time?

You combat that by constantly referring back to the living plan you are about to create and checking up on your progress.

Make note of what is working and what is not. Do not forget about the good parts, as we tend to only focus on what needs improvement. Those parts that are working well need just as much attention.

Spend some time in solitude when you complete this assessment. Take notes or record your thoughts on a voice recorder. Refer back to them over time. Why are certain parts not working as well? Are there similarities between them? Are they simply a case of getting used to a new behavior?

It is natural to feel uneasy when you are taking deliberate steps to change what in some cases may be deeply ingrained behaviors. Be patient with yourself while you change.

Try and do at least a partial review as soon as possible after you have tried a new strategy to deal with coworkers or your environment. Memories quickly fade or become distorted, so if you want change to come as quickly as possible, conduct your review as quickly as possible, too.

Some of the wordings are a little different to give you an additional way of looking at the question.

The topics will not be in the same sequence as they appear earlier as I want to create some logical groups of questions.

Grab a pen and notepad, folks. It's time to create your Motivation Living Plan.

1. Initial Assessment

Self-Care

This comes first, as no matter where you are and what you are doing, caring for yourself has to be a priority. Everything else we look at builds on this solid foundation.

- Are you eating healthy?
- Are you getting enough rest?
- Do you regularly exercise for at least 20 minutes?
- How are things progressing for you at work?
- Do you have any physical or mental concerns you need to bring up with a medical professional?

Care For Those Who Depend On You

Now look at your most important relationships. If you are married, it is your spouse. After that it is your children.

- Are you sufficiently providing for your family? Are their most important needs being met?
- Are you spending enough quality time with them?
- Are you showing genuine love and concern for them?
- How is your work/life balance?

Self-Assessment - Education

- What were your favorite subjects in school?
- What were your least favorite subjects in school?

Self-Assessment - Leisure Time

- What are your favorite leisure activities?
- Are they mostly enjoyed inside or outside?
- Are they solitary activities or done in a group?
- Do they involve physical activity or are they more sedentary?
- Are they in one set location or do you have to travel to different venues?
- Do the activities provide mental stimulation or do they allow you to "shut down" a bit?
- Are there individual tasks that are common to some or all of these activities?

Self-Assessment - Work Patterns

- After charting your output over several months, at what times of day are you most productive?
- When are you least productive?
- How can you plan your schedule so you are doing your most challenging duties during your peak periods?

Self-Assessment - Learning Style

Auditory Learners

- Do you read slowly?
- Does it take a long time for you to interpret complex pictures or detailed graphs?
- Do you enjoy talking to others?
- Are you a music fan, with a great memory for lyrics and bands?
- Is your preference for giving oral reports over written ones?

Tactics For Auditory Learners

- Try for a more isolated workspace away from elevators, telephones and main hallways.
- Secure earplugs, headphones or other noise cancelling devices to use when high levels of concentration are needed.
- Record meetings.
- Receive training on a CD or digital audio format.

Visual Learners

- Are you good at spelling but forgetful of names?
- Do you like pictures and charts?
- Do you like bold colors?
- Do you pay much attention to your fashion?
- Are you a hand talker?
- Do you take detailed notes?
- When people speak, do you make movies in your mind of their descriptions?

Tactics For Visual Learners

- Find space to "decompress" after important meetings.
- Take detailed notes at all meetings.
- Ask for written materials when possible.
- Sit across from main speakers whenever possible.
- Have face-to-face discussions whenever possible.
- Create maps or critical paths for projects.

Tactile Learners

- Do you enjoy having the radio on when you work?
- Do you enjoy doing two things at once?
- Are you a pacer during meetings, or wish you could be?
- Do you enjoy acting and visual arts?
- Are you good at sports?
- Is your hand-eye coordination above average?
- When learning something new, do you roll up your sleeves and get right into the middle of it?

Tactics For Tactile Learners

- Try and move around whenever possible.
- Exercise on breaks.
- Take frequent breaks when presented with large amounts of material.

Internal Focus Goals

- What are the personal goals that consistently drive you in every position you have been in?
- What are the most important results you want to see out of your work?

Others' Assessment - Those Who Know You Best Say...

- What are you doing when you are at your best?
- Which tasks give you the most trouble?
- Which activities seem to make you the happiest?
- What do they see as a great job for you and why?

2. Your Experience

Take every significant job, educational experience and volunteer position you have ever had and list them on one side of a page. Across from each position, write a detailed list of duties you completed in that role.

- What tasks appear on your experience list a lot?
- Do you enjoy those tasks?
- What types of jobs make good use of the skills you enjoy?

Workplace Motivators

On a scale of 1 to 6, with 6 being very important, how important are the following factors for you?

- Intellectual stimulation
- Variety
- Leadership opportunities
- Being around others
- Job security
- Prestige of the position
- Amount you are closely supervised
- Receiving attention
- Little if any extra hours required
- Presence of learning opportunities
- Large salary

3. Learning About What's Out There

Identifying Opportunities

- What types of jobs feature many of your favorite skills and workplace motivators?
- Do you know anyone in those careers?
- Have you asked your friends if they know anyone?

Taking Steps

Make lunch or coffee appointments with a few of these people to learn about what they do.

- Are there part-time or volunteer opportunities available in those careers?
- Are there business networking opportunities where you can meet people in those fields?
- Will you need additional education?
- Is that education available locally? By correspondence? Part-time? Online?
- How will you pay for any education?
- Can your family and lifestyle adapt to the added expense and time spent in school?
- Who can help, both financially and with their time?

Assessing The Market

- What are the job prospects in this field locally?
- What are the chances of you having to move to another place?
- Are you prepared to do that?
- What is the starting wage in your desired field?
- Can you afford to work for that wage?

Learning From Others

- Who are some of the successful people in your desired profession that you or your family and friends know?
- Identify one or two to keep in touch with on a regular basis so they can serve as a mentor to you.

4. Maximizing Your Current Position

Conduct your own performance review by using an existing job description or by developing one on your own. Be honest about your output in every area you contribute to.

Should I Stay...?

If after your review you realize your current position is not that bad, or if you will not be ready for the next step for a while, you need a plan so you can get as much as possible out of this job.

Workplace Accommodations

Are there any improvements to your physical workspace or any devices your employer can provide that would improve your work output?

Becoming More Productive

- Develop and constantly update a running to-do list.
- What do you do when you get bored or frustrated at work?
- Do you get distracted by internet surfing or other time-wasters?
- Would you benefit from accountability software or blocking websites?

Understanding Your Co-Workers

- What do you think are your main coworkers' preferred learning styles?
- Are their changes you can make to your behavior to help them?
- Is your workplace a socially active workplace?
- Are there opportunities to socialize with your coworkers outside of work?
- Who are the main influencers at work?

Or Should I Go?

- If you have determined it is time to leave, how can you make the most of the time left in your current job?
- What skills and experiences present in your current role could be used in your next step?
- How can you make those more a part of your role now?
- What skills and experiences that are needed in your next step could be part of your current role?
- What steps do you need to take in order to make some of these skills and experiences part of your current job?
- What short-term goals can you set that can keep you motivated to perform at your best?
- Which coworkers do you want as references?
- What short term external focus goals can you set to help you be productive during the remainder of your time in your current job?

~~~~~

Getting a much deeper sense of where you stand is what we're after with your Motivation Living Plan. When you do this exercise in an honest, dedicated, and complete manner, you will have your own personal paper accountability partner always at your side.

Introspection is just part of the bigger picture of figuring out what you really want to get out of your job and future. I know you're gaining a greater insight on where you are and where you want to go. Get ready from some interesting surprises with this new look into your professional development.

Chapter 10

And May The Motivation Be With You

Thank you for taking this journey of understanding. Like anything valuable one acquires, you will appreciate the results you achieve because you worked hard for it.

You read this book because at some level, you were not happy with your status quo. Perhaps this was your first real attempt at self-assessment or earlier tries did not work.

You first looked at your goals. I started with goals because I wanted you to always be aware of the end game while working through this process.

How often do we stop in the middle of something to ask, "Why am I doing this again?" before quitting because we do not have an answer.

Keeping your goals in mind helps us get through the momentary setbacks and struggles we encounter during the process.

With the goals fresh on your mind, we next looked at why you were getting bored at work. The simple answer is that the current situation does not match up with some of your goals.

That unease you felt that drew you to this book may have been because something was not quite right but you could not pin it down. We compared your goals to your current situation and looked for areas of disconnect.

Now that you realize there is a gap between where you wish to be and where you are, you're empowered by having developed a plan to improve things.

You'll also commit to keeping an eye to the future so you can incorporate the successful steps into your ongoing behavior. When done properly, this is a valuable set of skills that you can refer to whenever you find yourself in a rut.

Harlan Sanders had no choice but to subvert his hopes because he had to support his family. He may never have actually been aware of what his goals were at the beginning, but over time they became clearer at the service station when his mind finally had time to settle down.

Beginning small, the Colonel started serving food and discovered he enjoyed it. Experiencing some success, he gained confidence before a major setback.

He never lost sight of how good he was at it, and at a time when most people slow down, he was just getting started. Through trial and success, Colonel Harlan Sanders found what he wanted to do with his life and earned every bit of his success.

May you be just as successful and motivated with whatever path you choose.

Stay motivated at the work you choose to do and always remember the Chickenade.

About Richard N. Stephenson

I'm the elbow-grease behind richardstep.com, helping thousands discover more about themselves and their career paths daily. I've published several books on career development, personality testing, optimizing learning, and building strengths. I've also designed online self-discovery and career aptitude tests.

Cancer once knocked me down, the good Lord gave me a second chance, and now I want to help you use yours. I take the old career development fluff and turn it into tools you can use. I live to make resources that are guaranteed to help you in your career boosting journey.

I live near Houston, TX, with my extraordinary wife, adorable kids, and overgrown backyard.

Please feel free to contact me. I'm always looking for more career and life enhancing tips.

EMAIL: **mailto:richard@richardstep.com**
TWITTER: **http://twitter.com/rstephenson_**
VIDEOS: **http://youtube.com/rstephensonable**
ADDRESS:
PO Box 3395
League City, TX, 77574-3395

Books by Richard N. Stephenson

See my **Amazon Author page** for my latest books.

http://bit.ly/rnsamazon/

See my **blog author page** for my latest books overall.

http://richardstep.com/products/

Your Review Counts!

If you enjoyed this book, or got at least one golden nugget of usefulness out of it, would you mind sharing your experience with the rest of the world, please?

A 2 to 3 sentence summary of your thoughts is an awesome gift to others who see it. (I LOVE reading them, too!)

Please leave a review on this book's Amazon page:

http://bit.ly/rnsamazon

I'm an independent publisher and your review means a lot to other people considering this investment. It really does help when you share your thoughts and feelings.

Plus, I like the idea of my kids coming by my author pages in 20 years and seeing what the world had to say. I am forever grateful!

Thank you,
Richard N. Stephenson